John F. Kennedy

BY KATY S. DUFFIELD

The Child's World
childsworld.com

Published by The Child's World®
1980 Lookout Drive • Mankato, MN 56003-1705
800-599-READ • www.childsworld.com

Acknowledgments
The Child's World®: Mary Swensen, Publishing Director
Red Line Editorial: Editorial direction and production
The Design Lab: Design

Photographs ©: Cecil Stoughton/White House, cover, 1;
Corbis, 4, 7, 11, 19; Bettmann/Corbis, 8; Frank Turgeon Jr./
John F. Kennedy Presidential Library and Museum, 12;
Donald Wilson/John F. Kennedy Presidential Library and
Museum, 15; AP Images, 16; Cecil Stoughton/White House/
John F. Kennedy Presidential Library and Museum, 20

ISBN 9781503808676
LCCN 2015958442

Printed in the United States of America
Mankato, MN
June, 2016
PA02303

ABOUT THE AUTHOR

Katy S. Duffield has a BA in English
from the University of Illinois–
Springfield. She is the author of more
than 20 books for children and has
written both fiction and nonfiction for
many children's magazines.

Table of Contents

Kennedy was captain of the PT-109 boat.

Danger on the Sea

It was late at night in 1943. A wooden boat bobbed in the water. Jack Kennedy was the boat's captain. Kennedy and his 12-man **crew** were part of the U.S. Navy.

The United States was fighting in World War II. One of the countries it was fighting against was Japan.

Kennedy stared out at the Pacific Ocean. Suddenly, a shape appeared in the darkness. It was a Japanese ship. It was coming right at them.

Kennedy tried to turn the boat. But it was too late. The Japanese ship crashed into their boat.

The **jolt** threw Kennedy to the floor. But he was not badly hurt. He called for his men. Many were in the water. Some called back. Two did not. These two men died at sea.

Kennedy helped his men get back to the boat. But they were not safe there. The boat was sinking. The men saw a distant island. They would have to swim for it.

One man was hurt badly. Kennedy grabbed the strap of the man's life vest. Kennedy put the strap in his mouth. He began swimming. He pulled the man along with him.

The men swam for almost five hours. They were weak and tired when they reached the island. But Kennedy could not rest. He had to find help. Some of

Kennedy received a medal for his brave actions after the boat crash.

his men were hurt. They thought Japanese soldiers might come back. The Japanese might capture them.

For five days, Kennedy swam to nearby islands. He searched for boats. But he did not spot any.

Finally, the men met two **native** people who were scouts for an Australian spy. Kennedy carved a note onto a coconut shell. The scouts took Kennedy's note to the spy. The spy sent more scouts to rescue Kennedy and his men.

Kennedy became a hero. He would continue to help his country.

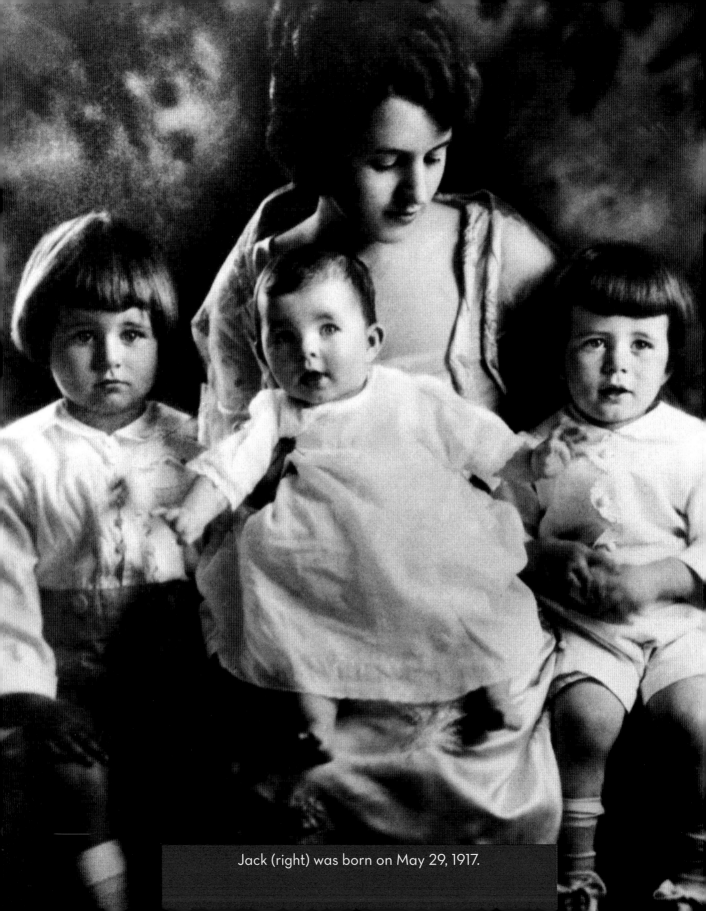

Jack (right) was born on May 29, 1917.

CHAPTER TWO

"Jack" Kennedy

On May 29, 1917, a baby was born in Massachusetts. His parents named him John Fitzgerald Kennedy. But his family called him Jack.

Jack was born into a wealthy family. He had eight brothers and sisters. The family lived a fun and comfortable life. Cooks prepared their dinners. They had picnics on the beach. They went sailing on sunny days.

Jack was a happy child. But he was sick a lot. When he was two years old, Jack got very ill. He had scarlet fever. His parents thought he might die.

Jack spent a lot of time in the hospital. But he finally got well.

When Jack was 14, he left home. He went to a **boarding school**. He was smart. He loved reading. But he didn't always work hard at school.

Jack had many friends. In his last year of high school, he received an honor. He was named "Most Likely to Succeed."

After high school, Jack went to college. He attended Harvard University. He played football there. He competed on the swim team. He played golf.

In 1938, World War II was fast approaching. Jack's father got a new job in England. Jack moved with his family. He had to leave Harvard. But he kept up with his studies.

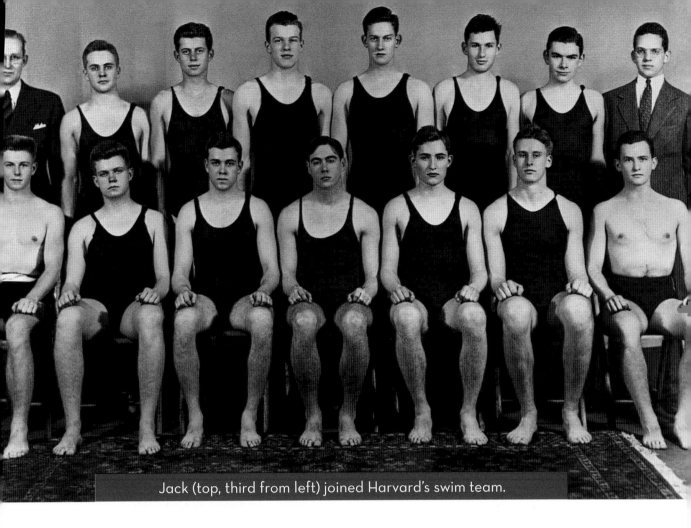

Jack (top, third from left) joined Harvard's swim team.

Jack traveled a lot. He went to places such as Russia and Poland. He visited France and Germany. Jack liked seeing new places. He wanted to know more about the world.

Jack returned home for his final year at Harvard. He graduated in 1940.

Kennedy served in the U.S. Navy from 1941–1945.

CHAPTER THREE

The Politician

After college, Kennedy thought about going to law school. But World War II was getting closer to home. Kennedy wanted to serve his country. So he joined the U.S. Navy in 1941.

Kennedy was proud to be in the navy. But life at sea was hard. He hurt his back in the boat crash. And he came down with a serious illness. Doctors gave him medicine. It kept his illness under control.

After he left the navy, Kennedy wrote for a newspaper. He wrote about world leaders. He wrote about the end of World War II. But he did not want to just write about world events. He wanted to be a part of them. So, in 1946, he turned to **politics**.

Kennedy hoped to become a member of the U.S. Congress. He spoke with voters. People liked him. In 1946, Kennedy won his first **election**. He was elected to Congress four more times.

Kennedy was often sick. Sometimes, it was hard for him to do his work. But he did not let that stop him.

Kennedy wanted to do more. He wanted to help the poor. He wanted to improve schools. He also believed that people should have equal rights. At the time, African Americans did not have the same rights as white people. They had separate schools. They could not use the same water fountains as white people. Kennedy hoped to change this. So he made a decision. In 1960, he ran for president.

LEADERSHIP FOR THE 60's

Kennedy ran for president in 1960.

Peace Corps volunteers help people in countries such as the Philippines.

CHAPTER FOUR

The 35th President

Some people did not think Kennedy should be president. Many thought he was too young. He was 43 years old. They thought he did not have enough experience. But others thought he was smart. They thought he had good ideas.

Americans voted on November 8, 1960. The race was close. But Kennedy won. He became the president of the United States.

Kennedy had many plans for the United States. He started the Peace Corps. Kennedy asked for **volunteers**. They would help people in other countries. They would teach others to read and write. They would help build roads. They would care for the sick.

Space travel was important to Kennedy, too. He wanted U.S. astronauts to be the first to land on the moon. He made sure the space program had money.

Kennedy also worked for **civil rights**. He thought all people should be treated the same. He believed African Americans and white people should be able to eat at the same restaurants. They should not have separate areas at the movies. But many people disagreed. These people made his work much harder.

Kennedy tried to keep Americans safe, too. The United States and Russia were **rivals**. They each wanted to be the most powerful country. They raced to see who could build the most weapons. In 1962, the Russians placed **missiles** in Cuba. Cuba is very close

OXIDIZER TRAILERS

OXIDIZER TRAILERS

The United States found evidence
of missiles in Cuba in 1962.

Kennedy visited Dallas, Texas, to campaign for reelection.

to Florida. The missiles were dangerous. They were aimed at the United States.

Kennedy worked hard to fix the problem. He spoke with the Russian leader. They had very different ideas. But they finally came to an agreement. Russia removed the missiles.

Kennedy had more work to do. So he ran for a second **term** in 1963. He went to Texas. He hoped Texans would help reelect him. Kennedy made speeches and met voters. He rode through the streets. The top of his car was down. A big crowd had gathered. Kennedy smiled and waved.

Then, gunshots rang out. Kennedy had been shot. He was rushed to the hospital. But doctors could not save him. Kennedy died from the wounds. He had been president for a little more than 1,000 days. But he had accomplished many things.

TIMELINE

1910

←— **May 29, 1917** John Fitzgerald Kennedy is born in Brookline, Massachusetts.

←— **June 1935** Kennedy graduates from boarding school.

←— **1938** Kennedy travels to many places around the world.

←— **1940** Kennedy graduates from Harvard.

←— **August 2, 1943** A Japanese ship rams the navy boat Kennedy commands.

←— **November 1946** Kennedy is elected to the U.S. Congress for the first time.

←— **November 1952** Kennedy is elected to the U.S. Senate.

←— **November 8, 1960** Kennedy is elected the 35th president of the United States.

←— **March 1961** Kennedy creates an organization called the Peace Corps.

←— **October 16, 1962** The United States confirms there are Russian missiles in Cuba.

←— **October 28, 1962** The United States and Russia agree to remove the missiles.

←— **November 22, 1963** Kennedy is shot and killed in Dallas, Texas.

1970

boarding school (BOHR-ding SKOOL) A boarding school is a school that students live at during the school year. Kennedy went to a boarding school.

civil rights (SIV-uhl RITES) Civil rights are rights that every person should have. Civil rights include the right to vote.

crew (KROO) A crew is a group of people who work on a ship under a captain's authority. Kennedy worked to protect his crew after the crash.

election (i-LEK-shun) An election is when people choose a leader by voting. Kennedy won his first election in 1946.

jolt (JOLT) A jolt is a quick and sudden movement. The strong jolt from the Japanese ship threw Kennedy to the floor.

missiles (MIS-uhls) Missiles are weapons that are thrown or launched at a target. Kennedy saw photos of missiles in Cuba.

native (NAY-tiv) Someone is native when he or she is born in a particular place. After his ship sank, two native people helped Kennedy get rescued.

politics (POL-uh-tiks) Politics are activities to gain or hold onto power in government. Kennedy joined politics in 1946.

rivals (RY-vuhls) Rivals are people who want the same thing when only one can have it. The United States and Russia were rivals because they both wanted to be the most powerful country in the world.

term (TERM) A term is the length of time an official can stay in office. Kennedy ran for a second term as president.

volunteers (vahl-un-TEERS) Volunteers are people who work without pay. People become volunteers in the Peace Corps to help the sick and poor in other countries.

In the Library

Krull, Kathleen. *The Brothers Kennedy: John, Robert, Edward.*
New York: Simon and Schuster Books for Young Readers, 2010.

Norwich, Grace. *I Am John F. Kennedy.* New York: Scholastic Inc., 2013.

Winter, Jonah. *JFK.* New York: Katherine Tegen Books, 2013.

On the Web

Visit our Web site for links about John F. Kennedy: **childsworld.com/links**

*Note to Parents, Teachers, and Librarians: We routinely verify our Web links to make
sure they are safe and active sites. So encourage your readers to check them out!*

INDEX